Uber Driving Pros and Cons:
Should You Become an Uber Driver?

Jason Moore

Jason Moore

Copyright © 2016

Copyright © 2016 Jason Moore
All rights reserved.
ISBN-10: **1523828757**
ISBN-13: **978-1523828753**

Topics:

INTRODUCTION

Uber is a "rideshare" company that allows customers to schedule, get picked up from and dropped off at predetermined destinations, entered using a smartphone app. One of the main advantages that this service offers over traditional Taxi Cab services is that one customer can request a ride and not pay multiple fees for taking groups of friends somewhere, hence "rideshare". You may also share a ride with a stranger for a cheaper fare.

The ease of scheduling, picking up, dropping off and paying the driver is a real game changer in the transportation industry and, because of this, there has been much news (both positive and negative) swirling around the company and some of its business practices. With a company valuation to the tune of billions of dollars, there are massive opportunities for improving the existing infrastructure to make things even better for Uber Drivers and customers.

The purpose of this book is to share my firsthand experience as a professional Uber Driver – or "Uberpreneur" as some folks like to call it – to help you decide if becoming an Uber Driver is for you or not. Driving has its ups and downs and, as you read this book, you will find out that it can be a lot of work. It is almost just as easy to become an Uber Driver as it is for the customer to order an Uber Driver.

WHY BECOME AN UBER DRIVER?

There are several reasons for becoming an Uber Driver, one of which is to earn supplemental or extra income besides your regular part-time or full-time job. You can work it as a side or main business and do it "full-time" if you want. The good thing about becoming an Uber Driver is that you work when you want to and you do not have to report to anyone. Please be advised that if you choose to become an Uber Driver, or run any business for that matter, you still have to answer to the customer, because they have the power to make your overall rating go up or down, which determines if you can remain a driver over the long-term.

The reason I chose to give Uber Driving a try is because I wanted to earn some supplemental income, in addition to my existing 9–5 position. Believe me, balancing driving for Uber (involving at least 30–40 hours a week) in addition to working a 9–5 (40 hours) position was no easy task. For example, I would get up at 4 AM sometimes and drive a few hours; drive on my lunch break and even after my day job at night until 12 AM during the week.

Your reason for considering becoming an Uber Driver might be different from mine but, whatever your reason, you should treat it as a business endeavor that can be fruitful if done properly.

HOW TO GET STARTED

Before you can even become an Uber Driver, you need a relatively new car in good-to-excellent condition, both mechanically and in physical appearance. If you have large dents in your car, you better go see Maaco to get those dents taken care of, as you might not get approved to drive. In most city markets, in the United States particularly, your car can be no older than four or five years old. If you can and if you are serious about becoming an Uber Driver, I highly recommend that you invest in either a hybrid or, if your market allows, an electric car, because gas will be one of your major business expenses.

Your personal background should be relatively squeaky clean, meaning no driving-related or violent felonies nor any non-driving violent misdemeanors. I have heard stories of folks with these types of criminal records getting through the system, but it is better to only apply to Uber if you don't have a history with the law enforcement at all.

If your car and background is good, just head over to: **https://get.uber.com/drive** to sign up and apply. You will need photocopies of the following items to upload to their website:

- Current Driver's License
- Current Registration
- Proof of Insurance
- Vehicle Inspection (Select city markets)

After you have completed the online paperwork application and uploaded the necessary documents, it usually takes a week to get processed and activated in the Partner App, which you will also download and install to your smartphone. This app allows you to receive nearby "pings", which are notifications that a customer needs to be picked up, in addition to managing transactions and mapping where to pickup and drop-off a customer.

CAR CLEANLINESS AND MAINTENANCE

Car preparation is a key determining factor of your success as an Uber Driver. Keeping a clean car is a must and it will negatively affect your rating if you fall short. First impressions matter and, if you don't want to be viewed as a sloppy and careless driver, always check the insides of your car before and after a pickup (if possible) to ensure cleanliness.

At least once a week, you might want to also consider spending $40 or more to have your car detailed and vacuumed by a professional car wash (it can't hurt). Not only should you make sure that the inner (seating) parts of your car are clean, but you also want to make sure that your trunk is free and clear of any large pieces of items, trash or junk that sometimes accumulates. You never know when you will get someone traveling with luggage for a trip to the airport, train or bus station, so it is better to play it safe with your trunk.

This is common sense, but sometimes taken for granted. Ensuring that your car is always in tip-top condition is a must if you want to help minimize potential performance issues and maximize the longevity of your vehicle. Make sure that you change your oil minimally after every 3,000 miles. Also ensure that you have tires in good condition or better and have regular tune-ups. In addition, you should never have any dashboard warning lights on when picking up customers. If a dashboard warning light comes on, be sure to get it checked out as soon as possible before picking up another customer. Paying attention to these few minor details can make a huge difference on the customer's overall perception of you, have an impact on their mood and, subsequently, your rating from that customer.

CUSTOMER SERVICE

Providing stellar customer service is key to keeping both you and your rating at a respectable level and making sure that there are no problems during a trip. At times, it may seem that, no matter how nice you are to a customer, they are not reciprocating your generosity. Perhaps they are having a rough day or they are in a bad mood for whatever reason. Your job, as a service provider, is to give them the best service possible and get them from point A to point B. Customer service is more than just doing your job. It is oftentimes going above and beyond the call of duty, so-to-speak, to ensure that the customer has a pleasant ride. Little things like asking them a few seconds after getting in, "How is your day going so far?" shows that you genuinely care about them and that you want to provide the best service to them. This can help your rating be a very positive one.

Other examples of providing good customer service include opening doors for your passengers and, of course, adjusting your seats if need-be for tall customers (do this without them asking for extra brownie points). You can never do too much when it comes to providing a stellar customer service. It can only help and not hurt your endeavors to become one of the best Uber Drivers because every rating counts.

WHAT TO WEAR

Your attire is also an important aspect of how you will choose to conduct business should you become an Uber Driver. It really comes down to your personality. I have heard of some drivers wearing button-down white shirts with a tie. It is a good idea to wear what is comfortable and, unless you think you are going to be picking up a lot of business people, then jeans and t-shirts on most warm days should suffice.

However, there are some types of attire that you should avoid, as they may come across as unprofessional. For example, wearing shorts in warm weather is a little too casual and might put some folks off. If the weather is hot, sandals for women may be acceptable but flip-flops would be overdoing it just a bit. The key is finding what you know most people will find as acceptable.

When in doubt about what to wear, you can never go wrong with a polo shirt and some slacks. Both men and women should consider this attire, as it is somewhat business casual and professional but conservative enough so you won't be looked upon as wearing inappropriate attire.

TOOLS YOU WILL NEED

Besides an up-to-date smartphone to use the Uber Partner App, there are some tools that will help you further, both as a driver and to get that extra ratings boost from the customer. These I refer to as "tools" but really, they are essentials, as customers are also rating you based on past driving experiences. Although there is no set way or standard that you must follow, because you are considered an Independent Contractor with Uber, there are certain items that you should at least consider having readily available.

One of the first tools that you should have in your arsenal is a backup GPS navigation device, in case your phone map navigation is unreliable or if it fails for whatever reason. Oftentimes a customer can and will point you in the right direction on how to get from point A to their destination; however, sometimes they may not want to. Always give them the upfront option. For example, ask, "Would you like to point the way to where you are going or would you like me to use GPS?"

The GPS question gives the customer the option and it is always much better to ask than assume that the customer wants you to find the way. Also, it helps to prevent disputes that you might have taken a longer route for some reason.

Having a portable car USB port, so that they can charge their phone or use a laptop, can come in handy and earn you extra brownie points and a higher rating. I have had customers ask if I had this. It is not a requirement; however, some drivers do provide this and customers may eventually grow accustomed to this extra feature.

On hot summer days especially, you can never go wrong with a cooler in the trunk with some water bottles. I have had a customer ask me for this as well and it can go a long way with helping to up your rating and providing better customer service.

DRIVING STRATEGIES

Being strategic about how much you work is just as important as knowing when to drive and sit and wait for a pickup ping. If you want to make the most money with Uber in the least amount of time, you should pay attention to the regular reports that Uber sends out about best driving times in your city.

You can easily spend 30–40 hours per week working while logged into the Uber App, but most of that is time is usually spent driving to "find" the best spots to get customer pings. The prime driving times in my city are typically Thursday through to Saturday nights, between 10 PM and 3 AM. However, you can make steady money driving customers throughout the day, albeit not as much as driving during the prime times.

The driving strategy that seemed to work best for me was to park near hotels (sometimes in their parking lots if they allowed) and wait for customers, rather than driving around looking for them. I'd find hotels or restaurants roughly 10 to 15 miles outside the main city, because there would almost always be customers wanting to drive back to the main metropolitan area.

The best trips for me were always runs to the airport, as you could easily rack up $45–$50 for taking someone to the airport for just one trip. The only catch to that is that you end up driving a 40–60 miles round trip just to get back near where you want to sit and wait for the best pings.

Saturdays and Sundays during the daytime were typically the best for getting back-to-back customer pings. That means it was so busy thosetimes that, as soon as I swiped "dropped off", I'd immediately get and accept a customer pickup ping to get someone else. You can also accept a ride if you are going in the same direction of another customer and the app seems to handle this well. Typically, you will only get a ping if the customer is 10 minutes or less away, but sometimes more if you are the only driver in the area.

HOW TO HANDLE YOUR FIRST CUSTOMER

If you have thoroughly paid attention to everything that I have written up to this point, there is no reason why you wouldn't receive a perfect 5.0-star rating from your first customer. As a matter of fact, you don't even need to tell your first customer that you are new, but gauge their interest in talking by using the icebreaker question, "How is your day going?" to see if they want to.

Some customers get so engaged in their phone or talking with another passenger that they almost don't know that you are driving them.

Respect also goes a long way and is a two-way street. Plus, you also get to rate a customer so, if the customer is out of line, you may also rate them appropriately. As a matter-of-fact, you get to see a customer's rating when they first ping you and so you can choose if you want to pick them up or not. Some customers want to be rated 5 stars almost as much as you should, so keep this in mind when rating them.

RECEIVING TIPS

At one time, technically speaking, you were not supposed to expect or solicit tips from Uber passengers. As a-matter-of-fact, the policy was that you were supposed to gracefully decline a tip at least twice before finally accepting if the customer insisted. However, I wouldn't personally argue with a customer. If a customer wanted to give me a tip, I didn't argue. Now, tips are part of the Uber app so tipping is no longer an issue.

PAYMENTS

With the help of a cutting-edge Uber partner website, you can login using your computer or phone and check your earnings, rating and miles driven up to the minute. If you need to know how much you can expect to make for the week, just login and look up your earnings. You are paid weekly through Uber or in real time as you earn if you have their debit card, which is one of the perks of driving with them. Best of all, there is no cap on how much you can make as a driver.

YOUR RATING

The rating system is one of the hotly contested aspects by drivers of the overall Uber experience. Your rating is a "quality control" mechanism used by Uber to determine if you will remain a driver. That is why it is *always* a good idea to do everything in your power to help ensure that you receive a 5.0 almost every time. Even a wrong turn here or there could negatively impact on a customer's rating of you which, of course, creates extra pressure on some drivers.

It is a known fact that, if your average rating falls below a certain threshold (for example 4.5), which by the way is still spectacular in some industries, you get deactivated as a driver and must go to the closest Uber branch, meet with someone and petition to get turned back on. Some drivers, including me, feel that the rating system needs a lot of improvement. For example, a weighted average of some sort that is based on ratings of those giving the ratings. That way, if a person with a low rating rates you lowly, then their rating does not count as much as someone with a higher rating.

While not perfect, I can see why the rating system is in place, but I hope that modifications are made to it so that it becomes more of a fair system to the driver. As subjective as it is, the threshold for being deactivated should be set much lower, as it is fairly easy to slip below the current threshold rating for the most minor issues.

SELECT DRIVING EXPERIENCES

One of my first "interesting" pickups was with a gentleman whom I picked up on a Thursday morning about 4 AM. He was doing the right thing by ordering an Uber, but it was evident that he had been drinking hard and later he revealed to me that he had taken some type of illegal substance too, so he was also acting a bit strange. He was relatively calm, though saying some odd things, but what really got me fired up was that he started smoking in my car. I said no problem and put down my windows so that the smell of smoke would immediately blow outside of the car. Smoking, eating and drinking in an Uber is not allowed, by the way. Once we got to his destination, he wanted to sit and chat about various topics in the slurred voice he had. I was just glad when he finally got out because of how odd his behavior was. I am sure you can only guess the low rating I gave him after it was all over.

Another "interesting" example was a Sunday morning pickup at about 6 AM. Three drunk people – two women and one man. The guy, apparently, was the owner of a pub in a popular area of town and he was "on a mission", so-to-speak. Luckily for me, they could at least partially hold their liquor and weren't as obnoxious as you would think. Both women were kind of flirty with me (at least one of them wanted me to go into the house with them) but I, of course, had to ignore it because I am married and wanted to remain professional. So, I eventually dropped them off at his house and he takes the six-pack of beer that he had with him (as if they needed it). To know the rest of the story after they got inside, you'd have to be a fly on the wall; however, in this case, three's company, four's a crowd!

Overall, my experiences were mild. I never had anyone throw-up in my car. Probably an obnoxious drunk customer here or there who insisted on eating in my backseat, but I was lenient because I wanted a good rating. It is better to give in and bend a little than getting into a confrontation or hurting your rating. You can always rate them accordingly if they get out of line a little. In my experiences with customers, from having numerous retail clients, I found that you usually get the behavior that you give. So, if you act professionally, 9 times out of 10, even if they have obnoxious tendencies, you can salvage the ride and they won't get too out of line.

BALANCING A RELATIONSHIP

Being in a relationship (in my case newly married), working a regular 9–5 and working Uber 30–40 hours a week as well was a challenge. As a matter of fact, it was a recipe for disaster. I was always tired from working two jobs. I could usually barely keep my eyes open when I watched television with my wife. Sometimes, I could barely stay awake at my regular day job.

I was motivated to make some extra cash but at what expense? To my relationship? My sanity?

There had to be a better way to make ends meet than what I was doing and my relationships were suffering due to the unbalanced nature of working so many hours. With Uber, you are away from home quite a bit and during the twilight hours too, when strange things can happen, so it is somewhat of a risk in more ways than one. For example, I have heard some people will throw up in your car if drunk enough, ewww! I also heard a horror story about an Uber ride to take someone for a drug deal.

In any case, balancing a relationship such as a new marriage with your significant other and a full-time job with Uber is a hard thing to do. It was extra money sure, but soon I began to see that, for me, the cons started to outweigh the pros.

GETTING PAID

The best part of being an Uber Driver is getting paid on a weekly/daily or real-time basis (depending on your payout option). Weekly, on Thursday early afternoons your payment will hit your bank account – if you are successfully signed up for direct deposit. Another good thing is that you never have to handle money when being a driver, which means that a would-be robber is less inclined to try to rob you for any money that you have collected during your work. All payments are done electronically, including tips.

MY EARNINGS (REVENUE)

On each trip, I averaged about $10. This means that, from the longer trips and shorter trips combined, my average trip was a mere $10. Remember, some trips only last 5 or 10 minutes and others can range between 20 to 30 minutes or more in the city. My first payment after working 40 hours was only $400 for one week. If I had been more strategic and worked only certain nights, in my city, I probably could have done that in 20 hours, commanding a nice $20 per hour worked. Hours worked is calculated by how much time you are logged into the app and are accepting customers. I have heard of someone on a long trip taking 8 hours or more and yielding over $1,000 in fares. It really depends on your market and a bit of luck or chance, along with some strategy which will determine how much you will make.

PROFIT

As any good businessperson does, you must calculate your profit. After you take all your revenue earned from your weekly payment, you subtract your expenses (such as gas, car maintenance, wear and tear on your vehicle, etc.) to determine your profit or what you are left with. That amount may surprise you and leave you wondering why you became a driver. However, if you drive a hybrid or an electric car, you will earn more profit than I have.

I will say that I have done only about 1000 trips over a year (off and on as a driver) and my feelings were mixed.

TAXES

A good perk about being an Independent Contractor with Uber is that you get to write off your expenses from your taxes. To do this successfully, you should consult a tax professional. You can write off things such as gas and car maintenance, etc.

On the other hand, you must pay income tax on your earnings because no funds are taken out of your pay. If you do it right, your write-offs will do a good job of offsetting your tax liability somewhat. However, be prepared to pay Uncle Sam his share when tax time comes.

COMMUNITY SUPPORT

Besides the Uber customer service, there is a range of community support options out there for new and existing drivers. There are countless YouTube videos with drivers sharing their experiences. There are also several Facebook groups; one of which is **Uber Man Driver Network** and a page named **Uber Driver Forum**, which is the Facebook Page for a popular Uber forum at www.UberPeople.net. Out of all these resources, I found YouTube videos and the Uber Driver Forum to be the most useful. Please keep in mind that there are a lot of negative comments from disgruntled drivers on the Uber Driver Forum, so take any advice you receive there with a grain of salt.

WOMEN DRIVERS

If you are a woman and are considering becoming an Uber driver, please be advised to take all necessary safety precautions. Even if you drive during the day, you never know if you will run into a lunatic. However, it can be done. I suggest that you put a camera in your car, even if it is fake to ward off any potential bad people. Or maybe carry a weapon or something that can be used as a weapon, that is your call.

If you are an average to above average looking female and you don't mind guys trying to hit on you, this may or may not be the right job for you. Also, you might want to require all passengers to always sit in the back seat and never up front with you but, if it is a group of four, then you may have a problem.

MY OVERALL OPINION

I firmly believe that Uber is a great service for customers, though the drivers could be respected a bit more internally speaking. Without drivers and customers, there is no Uber eco-system. The driver rating system needs an overhaul and the pay needs to be better in some cities. In a perfect world, Uber Drivers would have the freedom to drive whenever they wanted and could possibly be considered "dependent contractors" for the company.

College students and single adults just starting out on their careers are ideal as Uber Drivers, although some corporate professionals such as me also sometimes decide to take the plunge. Although it is good to have multiple streams of income or a backup job like Uber if you are a professional or have another job, balancing the time can also be a challenge.

www.ingramcontent.com/pod-product-compliance
Lightning Source LLC
Chambersburg PA
CBHW070309190526
45169CB00004B/1554